PRAISE FOR SHEILA PAXTON AND *GETTING PAST JADED*

"A heartfelt modern tale that reawakens faith in the search for love."

— J.L. Tracy, author of *Sincerely, The Mentor*

"*Getting Past Jaded* is a fantastic story that uses one person's journey to help you find your one true love."

— Brett Dupree, author of *Joyous Expansion: Unleashing Your Passion to Lead an Inspired Life*

"*Getting Past Jaded* can be your personal guide to loving relationships. Sheila's training and experience make her highly qualified to guide you through this journey."

— HC Joe Raymond, speaker, coach, and author of *Embracing Change from the Inside Out*

"Sheila has created the ultimate relationship guide. It combines well-written stories with practical tips to get you past jaded!"

— Robert Coorey, MBA, best-selling author of *Feed a Starving Crowd*

"What an inspiration! Relationships can be frightening, especially in the aftermath of a failed one. In *Getting Past Jaded,* Sheila Paxton gives you hope that you can truly find love and a relationship that meets your most intimate needs."

— Dr. Eric J. Scroggins, author of *Vision Blockers*

"*Getting Past Jaded* grabbed me from the beginning. Audra's journey is compelling and Lily is an amazing guide. They inspire the reader to stay grounded and mindful of day-to-day life—an important reminder for anyone!"

— Heather Allen, MGIM-MBA, author of
Let Your Creativity Work for You

"Anyone who's ever been ready to give up on love will want to give it another chance after reading *Getting Past Jaded*. From the first page, I was enticed by Audra's journey and Lily's practical and insightful advice, and I thought the ending was perfect. After reading this book, you'll feel both empowered and ready to embrace life again."

— Tyler R. Tichelaar, Ph.D. and award-winning author of
Narrow Lives* and *The Best Place

"Sheila Paxton has created a modern fable filled with deep insights that apply to anyone in today's fast paced but often unfulfilling world. Through her main character she takes you on a journey filled with self discovery and ultimately freedom to become one's true self. You will enjoy this journey and perhaps find yourself along the way."

— Jack Gallagher, author of *It's Your Choice*

"Sheila Paxton has captured the essence of a person who is burned out by relationships in *Getting Past Jaded*. The riveting story she tells is filled with insight and promise."

— Barbara Murray, MSW, LCSW,
author of *Taking Back Parenting*

This book will cure the hole in your heart while giving you hope and inspiration that your soul mate is still out there searching for you. If you have given up on finding true love, start here!

– Patrick Snow, International Best Selling Author of
Creating Your Own Destiny* and *The Affluent Entrepreneur

To Joel –
Wishing you
love & magic!
Sheila

GETTING PAST JADED

A Healing Parable of One Woman's Quest to Rediscover Love

Sheila Paxton

Getting Past Jaded
A Healing Parable of One Woman's Quest to Rediscover Love

Sheila Paxton
c/o Intentional Relationships
PO Box 20383
Boulder, CO 80308
www.IntentionalRelationships.com
www.Fit4Love.com

ISBN: 978-1-940984-09-4
Library of Congress # 2013923179

Editor: Tyler R. Tichelaar
Cover Design: Ingrid Muller and Fusion Creative Works
Jacket Design: Fusion Creative Works
Interior Book Fusion Creative Works, www.fusioncw.com

Every attempt has been made to source properly all quotes.

Printed in the United States of America.

Published by Aviva Publishing
Lake Placid, NY
518-523-1320
www.avivapubs.com

First Edition

For additional copies visit:
www.Fit4Love.com
www.GettingPastJaded.com

DEDICATION

To my husband, Orley Paxton: Your belief in me has kept me moving forward, even when I couldn't believe in myself; you've loved me unconditionally, and have encouraged my growth over these twenty-seven years. You have my heart forever.

To John and Natalie Tyler: Your guidance and relationship modeling showed me that with the right tools, amazing relationships are not just a dream—they're a reality.

To Jan West and Mike Connolly: Thank you for being the best business partners a person could ask for and for your support and encouragement along the way.

To my Fit4Love clients: You've inspired me, touched my heart, and have challenged my beliefs about relationships. Without you, this book would not have happened.

To my bonus daughter, Julie Nirvelli, and beautiful granddaughter, Dezi: You've shown me what complete love looks like, and have been a special part of my healing journey.

ACKNOWLEDGMENTS

I would like to recognize and thank the following people for their support, encouragement, and belief in my dreams. I would also like to thank all of those listed here who have helped me with this book, and with my coaching career.

Karen Bernardi, Lazer Brody, Annette Carpien, Ginger Cooley, Mike Connolly, Frankie Doiron, Donna Fox, Susan Friedmann, Andrea Gold, Chris Guerriero, Jon Hunsaker, Annette Ludwick, Ira Ludwick, Sid Ludwick, ZZ Ludwick, Liz Mandel, Ingrid Muller, Susan Ortolano, Orley Paxton, Dottie Ricketson, Robin Sharp, Shiloh Schroeder, Patrick Snow, David Steele, Tyler Tichelaar, Lynne Troupe, Mandy Walker, Cheryl Walters, and Jan West.

CONTENTS

Introduction

DO YOU HAVE A BROKEN PICKER?

Are you jaded and ready to give up on ever having a great relationship? If you are, I don't blame you. I know I was, which I'll tell you about later.

Look around—what do you see? Divorce rates are rising, marital dissatisfaction is at an all time high, and people are experiencing general relationship malaise. Our model for finding and keeping loving, healthy relationships is broken and needs to be fixed.

Have you ever been in love when something tragic happened? Have you lost faith in your ability to find true love? Are you feeling jaded about ever having the kind of relationship you've dreamed of having? Or are you just about ready to give up on love?

I've been in your shoes. It seemed like I kept picking the same types of partners, just in different bodies. It's okay to feel like you want to give up, but I wrote this book so you would know you're not alone; there is a way out, and I invite you to discover it here.

As I thought about how I'd like to present my approach to finding true and lasting love, I chose to write a parable. People learn through stories, and I wanted to be able to guide you better with two important characters: Audra and Lily.

Over the next seven chapters, you'll journey with the courageous Audra and the wise guide, Lily. Untie your shoes and step into Audra's. Read this book from her perspective. You'll get the most out of it that way.

Along the way, Lily, the guide, will highlight the most important discoveries that Audra makes in her personal and intimate journey. You'll find activities and resources to help you make these same discoveries, which will lead to finding true and lasting love.

I challenge you to make this book your personal road map to finding love. Allow it to be your tool to see what the ultimate relationship is all about.

So, you may be asking, "Who is Sheila Paxton, and why did she write this book?" I have been married and divorced twice, so I have felt like a complete relationship loser. After the second divorce, I realized I was the common denominator in all of my relationship problems, and I needed to find out what it would take to reverse my losing streak.

I met with relationship experts, went through therapy, took graduate programs, and was certified as a relationship coach. I realized I was missing some simple things, so I learned how to fix them. Oh, and most importantly, I met the love of my life along the way. We've now been married for more than twenty-five years and are best friends and true partners—we're still thrilled to be with each other.

I have devoted my life to helping people have the same relationship success I have been able to experience. I am a love and relationship expert and coach, and my life's mission is to decrease the rising divorce rate in our country and to increase loving, lasting relationships. I have put together a proven system with which I have helped thousands of people find the relationships they have dreamed of having.

I understand your apprehensions. You may not believe that love is real because you, too, are jaded. I want you to know that it's okay to feel that way. I'd like to challenge you to open your heart to what could be, and allow Audra, Lily, and me to guide you.

I want to be your coach, mentor, and accountability partner. Are you ready? Let me be your guide to *getting past jaded*. I invite you to begin your journey with us now.

Enjoy!

Jaded: fatigued by overwork; worn-out, exhausted, tired, and weary. The end result of a steady flow of negative experiences, disappointment, and lack of fulfillment.

Chapter One

DANCING KOI

Audra looked at her computer screen one last time before getting ready to leave work. She had promised herself that she was not going to check that online dating site again today, but she couldn't help it. She found herself clicking on one of her "Favorites," YourChoice.com, to see whether there were any responses to her messages.

Audra thought she wasn't too attached to these dating sites, yet she was quite disappointed when her mailbox was empty. This morning, Audra had "winked" at several guys, but once again, she got the same disappointing results. "Figures. They were all probably losers like usual," she said to herself.

It was not uncommon for Audra to be the last one to leave work these days. She hated going home to her empty house, so she checked her email, did some casual online shopping, and played another game of solitaire. She got one more bottle of water from the company fridge and pinched the dead leaves off the jade plant on her desk. But Audra's attempts at distraction could not mask the consuming emptiness inside her.

This evening, Audra was especially angry about going home alone. The silence was too much for her to handle today. She blamed her most recent ex-boyfriend, Terry, for the silence, her anger, and the emptiness.

It had been eight months since Terry had walked out of her life, yet Audra continued to replay their final conversation over and over in her head. She didn't understand what he had meant by "needing space." He'd had plenty of independence in their relationship. He'd gone biking with his friends, had a beer with colleagues after work, and took out-of-town trips whenever he wanted.

Audra had been sure Terry was "the one," but this relationship had ended like all the others. "One more disappointment; one more rejection; one more lousy choice," she muttered.

As Audra thought about Terry, she was reminded of her ex-husband Steven, whom she had divorced just before meeting Terry. "How is it possible that I keep making these lousy choices? Forty years old and clueless about relationships," she thought.

As she slipped deeper into a dark pool of self-pity, Audra heard a chime from her smartphone. She picked it up and gazed at the screen. It was another text from Terry. "What does he want from me?" She could feel herself getting angry and excited at the same time whenever he texted her. She thought about deleting the note without reading it, but she couldn't resist the temptation.

"What a bunch of crap—another, 'How are you doing?'" Audra fumed at the phone and sent an abrupt response. "Is this what you mean by space? Can you just leave me alone?" she typed forcefully. "You said it was over, but you keep checking up on me all the time. Is it over, or what?" One long minute later, the phone chimed again. "Give me a break—just seeing if you're OK. Forget it." The usual ending.

Audra was tired of the game, and angry, too. Maybe it was her anger that propelled her into making a surprising declaration as she faced the green glow of her computer. "That's it. I give up. I have no idea what I'm doing when it comes to men." Audra felt some relief as she made that statement to herself; it was like she was able to tuck her frustration into a little emotional compartment and wrap up her day.

As she organized her desk, Audra was fueled by her new awareness. "I'm going to declare my freedom this evening," she thought. She was at a turning point—she couldn't keep going forward like this, and she certainly couldn't go back to the way she had been.

Audra had a history of impulsivity in all aspects of her life. A coworker had given her a book about emotional restraint several months ago. Audra consumed the contents and started practicing new strategies, like pausing for fifteen minutes before making important decisions. However, this evening, Audra was on an emotional mission and she simply wanted to push forward into something new without delay. Audra's declaration of freedom was going to be a tattoo—and she wanted it now.

Throwing her jacket over her shoulder and turning off the light, Audra remembered seeing a tattoo shop a few blocks from her home, so she started toward it. The street was alive with people hurrying to get home. She wondered how many others would be walking into an empty house. Audra looked at the faces of strangers, thinking that every person she saw probably had his or her own demons to deal with, yet she still felt alone with hers.

Audra rounded the corner of Walnut Street and passed the familiar old stores. Most of them had faded signs and iron gates protecting their contents. She zipped her jacket in the cool of the evening air and walked a little faster to stay warm. She longed for a time when people didn't have to live or work in fortresses.

Audra's ruminating was interrupted when she found her destination. It was a small shop with leaded glass windows that were covered with metal security bars. An old-fashioned sign hung just above the narrow door, painted with colorful art that resembled a tattoo of two fish swimming in a yin/yang circle. The name painted underneath it read, "The Dancing Koi Body Art Salon."

"Dancing Koi," Audra mused. She was instantly taken back to a business trip two years ago when she'd had an assignment in Japan. In the hotel lobby had been a koi pond, teeming with brilliantly colored fish. Audra had lingered by that pond numerous times during her stay.

A placard next to the pond had described the koi's significance, "According to Japanese legend, if a koi succeeds in climbing the falls at Dragon Gate on the Yellow River, it will be transformed into a dragon. Based on this legend, the koi has become a symbol of perseverance in adversity and strength of purpose."

Audra snapped out of her daydream and smiled as she looked up at the pastel picture of the dancing koi. She thought, "This is exactly where I'm supposed to be."

As she opened the smoky glass door, Audra heard the sound of an electronic gong, announcing her arrival. A petite woman appeared from the back of the salon. Audra heard the faint sound of Japanese music in the background. The air smelled like rubbing alcohol mixed with jasmine incense.

The proprietor came forward to greet Audra, "Welcome to The Dancing Koi. I'm Lily. How can I support your journey?" Audra thought that was a rather strange, yet comforting question.

"I'd like to get a tattoo this evening. Do you have time?" Audra asked.

"I'm free now. Do you have a design in mind?" Lily replied. She was dressed in black yoga pants with a flowing yellow tunic. Her long black hair was pulled back in a tight braid. Audra noticed that Lily did not wear makeup, yet her skin glowed with a radiance that seemed to emanate from somewhere deep inside.

As Audra took in her surroundings, she noticed that Lily had several large and colorful tattoos that were visible through her gauzy tunic. Something peaceful and comforting about Lily drew Audra in. As she became more comfortable with Lily, Audra's commitment to get a tattoo strengthened.

Before tonight, Audra hadn't thought of herself as the tattoo type. Something about declaring her independence heightened her resolve to wear her independence on her body.

"What design do you want?" Lily asked.

Audra panicked for a moment because she hadn't thought that far. "I'm not sure. Actually, I just decided to do this about an hour ago. Do you have some suggestions?" Audra replied.

"Look at the walls; all my art is there," Lily said. Audra began to walk around the shop and was mesmerized by the visual feast of colorful tattoo designs. As she gazed at the possibilities, her eyes landed on a colorful picture of a dragonfly. It was deep azure blue with iridescent jade and turquoise wings. The image appeared to be floating off the wall.

"This is it," Audra said. "I love it."

"Are you sure?" Lily asked. "You're making a long-term commitment when you get a tattoo."

"That's it. No question. It's speaking to me and I'm drawn to it. That's enough for me," Audra insisted.

"Well then, do you know what the dragonfly means?" Lily asked.

"Not really," Audra replied.

"It takes a special type of person to be able to wear the dragonfly. You must have a sense of freedom and an ability to change direction quickly. You also need to understand your values and always move toward them, no matter what happens," Lily explained.

Audra was excited about the dragonfly's significance and knew it represented qualities she wanted to develop. "This is exactly what I need," Audra said, sounding more confident than she really felt about her ability to develop a sense of freedom and fluidity.

"Let's get started," Lily said excitedly. She gathered up her tools and changed the tip in her new tattoo machine—the Impala. Lily thought about using her older machine because she wasn't yet familiar with all the workings of the Impala. After some thought, however, she decided this was the right piece of equipment for the job.

Lily carefully filled each of the small inkwells with various shades of purples, blues, yellows, and greens. She opened several sterile packages of gauze swabs and lined them on a stainless steel tray. Audra watched with a childlike curiosity mixed with a healthy dose of fear.

As Lily finished her preparations, she asked, "Where do you want the dragonfly?"

Audra thought for a moment and responded, "Let's do it on my forearm. It'll be easy for me to see so I don't forget about the promise to myself."

Lily gently cleansed Audra's forearm with rubbing alcohol. The pungent smell caught Audra by surprise. "You'll feel some slight stinging as I work. Just let me know when you want a break," Lily said gently.

Lily picked up the machine and turned on the switch. A high-pitched buzzing filled the room as Lily started her art. As the metal tip met the surface of Audra's skin, there was a loud, whining noise. Lily was startled as the tattoo machine's tip bounced off of Audra's skin like a rubber ball bounces on pavement. Lily thought something was wrong with the equipment. She turned it off, removed the inkwells, and looked for the problem. Everything seemed to be fine. She started the machine again, but she had the same result—the ink could not penetrate Audra's skin.

"I've only seen this happen once before," Lily whispered. "Three years ago, I was trying to tattoo a young man whose dog had just died. Actually, he brought in a picture of his dog so I could tattoo it onto his shoulder. When I started to work, I had the same strange experience as I just had with you. I couldn't get the ink under his skin. It's as if he had built a shell around himself."

"What happened?" Audra inquired.

"I don't know. He left and I never saw him again. My sense is that he was so wounded that he built an impenetrable emotional wall around himself. Those are really tough to tear down, and it's almost impossible to remove them alone. Can you relate to any of this?" Lily asked.

Audra leaned back and sighed deeply. She felt defeated and confused. "Why is everything so hard?"

"I'm starting to have a sense about you, Audra. Do you know what your name means?" Lily asked.

"No," Audra replied cautiously.

"It means 'inner strength,' but there's something in you that's conflicting with who you were meant to be," Lily responded. "I think there are some important things you haven't released, and you've closed yourself off from emotional connections, especially love. Am I on target?" Lily asked gently.

Audra felt her stomach tighten as Lily spoke. How did this woman already know so much about her? It was both scary and exciting. "You can't believe how right you are. I'm stuck, and this tattoo was an attempt to assert my independence and freedom. What do I do now?" Audra asked.

"Let me tell you a story," Lily started. "It's about the impala. That's why I picked that brand of tattoo machine," she said as she pointed to the equipment. "An impala can jump thirty feet forward, or higher than ten feet, yet it can be restrained behind a three-foot fence."

Audra wondered where Lily was headed with this story. What did an impala have to do with her?

Lily continued, "You see, an impala will not jump unless it can see where its feet will land. The landing spot must be completely visible."

Audra knew she was similar to the impala. She had allowed herself to be constrained by so many things that she had lost her confidence in the world around her. She wasn't open to anything unknown.

Audra was shaken by the events of the past half-hour. She had never met this person, yet Lily seemed to be able to see inside her. "So, I'm a bit like the impala and the guy you couldn't tattoo. Now what?" Audra asked.

Lily sat down next to Audra. She took a sip from the china teacup that was placed precariously on a small wooden table next to her. As she drank the tea, Lily spoke softly. "About fifteen years ago, I was with the man of my dreams, and I had planned to spend the rest of my life with him. Several months after we moved in together, he came home drunk. We got into an argument and he pushed me down the stairs. I was shocked by his brutality, but I immediately went into denial about his intention. 'He couldn't have really meant to do this,' I thought.

"I laid motionless on the floor, taking inventory of my body. As I did an internal scan, I realized my wrist was broken. We went to the hospital and I lied about how I had hurt myself. The next day, my boyfriend was apologetic, and he even cried, claiming he didn't know what had come over him, but it was probably the alcohol. I stayed with him for another two years and suffered through six more episodes of abuse," Lily admitted quietly.

Audra wondered how this person in front of her, who seemed so compassionate and knowledgeable, could let herself be hurt like that.

"I hit an emotional bottom," Lily continued. "I grew to hate that man, but I hated myself even more for not being able to take care of myself.

"One day, my yoga instructor pulled me aside after a class. She told me she was concerned because I seemed increasingly distressed, and I was losing a lot of weight. We sat and did a meditation together where it became crystal clear what had happened to me. I had lost myself. I could go on and on and tell you about my childhood, and my challenges, but the bottom line is I lost myself, and I committed then and there to finding my way back," Lily declared.

"I went back home and had a terrible fight with the jerk. I walked out the door and never looked back. I moved here to get some distance, and then I began my inner journey. I worked with some of the most amazing people, who helped me get to this place. I never knew I could feel so strong, or be so clear about what I need and want. I was guided to take my artistic talents and touch others. Audra, I'm open to life now, and I am not afraid to meet it head on," Lily affirmed.

"The most important discovery I made was finding out who I am, not who someone else wants me to be. I know what I want, and I believe I'm worth it," Lily said with confidence. She continued, "Take a look at the quote over my door. It's from John Emmons: 'Faith is the ability to trust what we cannot see, and with faith, we are freed from the flimsy enclosure of life that only fear allows to entrap us.'

"Audra, I stopped needing to be in love; then I discovered love. I stopped trying to find 'the one,' and then I met the one. We've been together for six years and the relationship works. It really works at all levels," Lily said.

Audra wanted what Lily had—faith in herself and her life. She ached with a longing she had never felt before as the notion of becoming open to life sunk in. "I want to be able to wear the dragonfly. I want the freedom and independence. I want the kind of faith you have. What do I do?" Audra asked.

"You know, I didn't plan on meeting you, but I was open to it," replied Lily. "I'm simply a tattoo artist who has been on her own journey, and I try to help others by sharing what I've discovered."

"Can you give me some guidance? I just need to know where to start," Audra pleaded.

"Let me ask you this, and please think before you answer," Lily responded. "Do you really want to know what's causing you to be closed to your life and to love? Your shell can't be penetrated, and opening up will be very challenging. I'm not sure you'll be able to get to the place where you're open enough to wear the dragonfly."

"Tell me how to start, please," Audra pleaded. "I'm ready."

"If you're truly ready, your journey will reveal itself. Start with a small step of faith. Believe that your journey will unfold as it should. That's all I know. Come back as you discover who you're meant to be," Lily said softly.

Audra replied with a willingness that was new to her. "I'm ready, and I will accept that my journey will unfold as it should."

Audra gathered her jacket and purse and went out into the night.

Lily: *Audra's just started a bold, new journey, and so have you. In Chapter One, she makes four life-changing discoveries. Please take a few minutes to review each discovery; then write about how each one applies to you. We'll do this after each chapter, so you, too, will experience the kind of transformation Audra experiences.*

Discovery 1: Audra realized she was fed up with the status quo. She didn't want to continue living the same way, but she didn't know what to do next. Describe how this situation relates to you:

Discovery 2: Audra decided to mark the beginning of her new-felt independence by getting a tattoo. What might you do to mark the beginning of your journey toward finding true love?

Discovery 3: It was clear that Audra had built an emotional wall around herself to protect her from being hurt, but that wall has also kept everything out. Have you built any invisible walls around you? Please describe them and think about how they developed. Are you ready slowly to start taking them down?

Discovery 4: Without knowing it, Audra had lost herself, and now she realizes she needs to take action to rediscover who she is. Are there any parts of yourself you feel are lost and need rediscovery?

Chapter Two

JOURNEY TO JADED

The next morning, Audra woke early, disoriented and confused. It was one of those mornings when she couldn't remember what day it was. Memories of last night's encounter with Lily flooded her thoughts, while images of tattoos danced before her eyes. She quickly remembered that it was Saturday, which shifted her troubled mood. Audra knew she would have difficulty concentrating at work after what she had experienced, so she was grateful she had the weekend to process what had happened.

Audra decided to hike to her favorite spot. She dressed in her most comfortable workout clothes and reached for her well-worn hiking boots. As she laced the sturdy shoes, Audra realized her mood was quickly shifting to one of calm and gentle anticipation. She loved to hike and always felt more serene at "her" lake. She filled her water bottle, then grabbed a protein bar, and headed out the door.

The early morning sun cast dancing shadows on the path that was so familiar to Audra. The air was fresh so Audra breathed in deeply. "This is just what I need," Audra thought. "I can't make sense out of what I discovered last night. Am I so blocked that I don't even know it?"

Audra began to see the sparkling lake's banks as she made her way up the rock steps built into the trail. Her legs felt strong and she breathed the cool air deep into her belly as she climbed. As Audra approached the last stone step, she saw the serene lake. It was crystal blue and surrounded by yellow and purple wildflowers. She made her way to the lake's narrow edge and sat on a rock she had named "Inspiration Point" many years ago.

Audra closed her eyes and focused on the sounds that surrounded her. Meadowlarks sang in the distance and aspen leaves rustled in the soft breeze. Her special rock felt cool and solid under her. As she felt her body relax, Audra heard a gentle buzzing. She opened her eyes to marvel at what she saw. Three dragonflies hovered just in front of her. She could see their double pairs of translucent wings sparkling in the sunlight. The dragonflies seemed to dance in the breeze; then as quickly as they appeared, the mysterious creatures flew away.

Audra felt oddly alone, even here at her favorite spot. "Have I really built a wall around myself?" she asked out loud. "I didn't know it was there, but I have the feeling that it's been there for a long, long time." Audra's spirits sank.

Just then, the breeze picked up, and Audra noticed that it created ripples on the sparkling lake's surface. As she looked at the swirling water, Audra saw that the ripples were organizing into the graceful shape of an impala. When the majestic animal started to speak, Audra pinched herself to see whether she was dreaming.

"I've come to start you on a journey," the impala said. "Lily told you that I can't take risks and my movements are measured and limited to only what I see," the creature continued. "My fear keeps me from being free and there's nothing I can do. I haven't been given the capacity to change. You have that gift. You have the ability to choose a very different path, but you don't see it," the animal said.

Audra fought the message she was hearing. She felt confused and didn't know what to do next. She noticed she had been holding her breath, so she relaxed her body to take in the cool air. As she relaxed a bit, Audra noticed the sky was turning a deep azure. She sensed she was on a journey that would change her completely. At that moment, Audra realized her world had changed forever and there was no turning back.

The impala dissolved into the lake and was replaced by an image of Audra as a young girl. Audra witnessed her younger self running into her bedroom to hide under her bed, as her father rampaged through the house. Young Audra had a love-hate relationship with this man. He would push her away when he was angry, but act lovingly when he was calm. As Audra watched this scene, she realized she had started to build her emotional wall when she was just a child. She had been inside the wall for a very long time—so long that it seemed to be a natural part of her.

The image in the lake then transformed into a scene from Audra's marriage to Steven. They were sitting by this same lake, arguing about having children. Audra could see the man she had once loved. She had believed that he cared about her, but he had always put his own needs first, no matter what it might cost the relationship. He went from job to job because his employers "didn't understand him."

Audra had worked hard to support the couple, thinking it would help keep peace in their household. She realized she had always come to the rescue when Steven was in trouble because she simply wanted normalcy in their relationship. She desperately needed to be needed and would do anything to have Steven depend on her.

Audra felt sick as she watched her relationship with Steven unfold before her. "Of course I needed to emotionally detach. I just sold my soul," Audra thought. She was ready for this dream to end. But there was more. Once again, the breeze shifted, and Steven's image morphed into her father's. Audra had the disturbing realization that she had married a person who was emotionally just like her father, even though she had done her best to push her father out of her life.

Audra's breathing quickened. More images appeared in the water. Audra tried to turn away, but she found she couldn't take her eyes off what she was seeing. She saw the figures of all of her past lovers and noticed that a black rope connected them all. All of these men shared the common bond of being emotionally unavailable and irresponsible.

Suddenly, the breeze stopped and Audra lay back on the rock, exhausted. Later, she had no idea how long she had lain there. She had let the images wash over and through her. Finally, she realized all she could see in the lake were the reflections of aspen trees and puffy white clouds.

"I have no idea how to pick a partner. I just keep repeating my past," she thought with a sense of resignation. Audra started quietly to cry as her emotional dam broke. She couldn't remember the last time she had let herself cry, yet now she had no choice. The floodgates had been raised and Audra released years of sadness and shame.

When there were no tears left, Audra composed herself, sat up, and noticed that she felt defeated, but excited at the same time. She felt cleaned out inside and had a glimmer of hope that, just maybe, seeing these patterns could help her with the wall, though she couldn't sort through just how that might work. She quickly stood up and began her hike back to town to pay another visit to Lily and tell her what had happened.

Lily was just opening up the Dancing Koi for the day ahead. Audra smelled tea brewing in a pot by the front desk and saw Lily straightening her tools. "Come on in," greeted Lily. "I made enough tea for two. Want to join me?"

"I'd love a cup," Audra said. "Do you have time to listen to what just happened to me?" Audra hoped Lily didn't have an early appointment so she could talk to her for a few minutes.

Lily noticed that Audra seemed agitated and invited her to sit down on the padded bench against the front wall. "I have time. No hurry. What happened to you? You look amped," Lily said.

Audra shared her story with Lily, describing every image she saw. Lily listened intently, leaning in toward Audra as she spoke. "So what I realized hiking back," Audra whispered, "is that I'm clueless about picking a partner. My relationship picker is broken," she said with resignation.

Lily smiled and chuckled gently. "I'm not finding this funny!" Audra exclaimed.

"I'm not laughing at you," Lily responded. "I'm just thrilled that you've discovered you don't know what you're doing when it comes to love."

"Well, I'm not thrilled. I'm frustrated and upset, mixed with being pissed at myself."

"Audra, lighten up a little on yourself," Lily said gently. "Don't you think you did the best you could with the tools you had? You've selected every guy in your life for some reason, and you're just starting to understand those reasons."

"It seems like I've been trying to resolve some issues I had growing up in a household where there was always emotional pushing and pulling," Audra replied.

"Exactly! Each relationship has served you in some way to help you get to this place, right here, right now. You're starting your journey of healing and learning!" Lily exclaimed. "Something in me senses that you have removed some of your emotional barriers. Do you want to give that dragonfly another chance?"

"Absolutely," Audra said excitedly.

Lily set up her equipment and once again filled the inkwells with vibrant colored inks. She placed the tattoo machine on Audra's skin and completed the dragonfly's tail. As Lily began the dragonfly's midsection, the machine stopped again. Lily was not surprised this time.

"That's all you're ready to accept," Lily said. Audra was disappointed because she thought she had discovered the key to what was closing her off. "You've started a really complex journey. Understanding why you've made certain choices is just one piece of your work. There's more to come," said Lily. "Some of your wall is coming down, but I sense there's a lot left."

Audra had to agree.

Lily: *Audra's already made some amazing discoveries, and I'm sure you have, too. Let's take a look at her four new ones and see how they apply to you.*

Discovery 1: Audra realized that fear of the unknown, or of upsetting the status quo, has kept her from being free. Describe how this realization relates to you:

____

____

____

____

____

____

____

____

Discovery 2: Audra realized she has compromised herself and her needs by avoiding conflict and trying to be the peacemaker. Have you experienced this situation? Please describe how it has appeared in your life.

____

____

____

____

____

____

____

____

Discovery 3: As Audra described her past relationships, she started to see significant similarities. Think about your past significant relationships. For each one, describe why the relationship did not work. Then go back through your writing and highlight the similarities across the relationships.

Discovery 4: Audra admitted that she had a broken relationship picker. Describe how you relate to that statement.

Chapter Three

VISIONS IN A CRACKED MIRROR

Audra was daydreaming when Zac approached her desk. She jumped when he entered. “Sorry; it looks like I scared you,” Zac said. “Boy, you were out there. Just wanted to see if you want a cup of coffee. It’s my turn to fetch.”

“I’ve been a little jumpy lately,” Audra responded. “I had some weird stuff happen over the weekend. No big deal, but it’s been taking up a lot of space in my head,” Audra said. “I’d love a large coffee.”

As Zac walked out of her office, Audra noticed she had been rapidly tapping her toe on the floor—she was frustrated and impatient. It was hard for her to accept that she had compromised herself in all of her romantic relationships, yet the facts were evident. Audra was puzzled and annoyed that she had let it happen again and again.

“I’m just an imposter,” Audra thought. “I put on this act with men like I’m open to a relationship, but I’m not. I’m closed off and don’t have a clue about what to do next.”

As she sank deeper into self-pity, Audra looked across her office and noticed that her antique framed wall mirror had a large crack running diagonally through it. “How the hell did that happen?” she fumed. “It must have been those cleaners again. Nothing’s safe in here." Audra believed that the cleaners had probably knocked the mirror off the wall, broken it, then had the nerve to hang it back up without letting her know what had happened.

Audra pushed back her chair and walked over to inspect the mirror. As she approached it, she locked eyes with the vision she saw. She realized she had never looked herself directly in the eyes in any mirror. When she put on makeup or checked her clothes, Audra looked at a reflected vision, but she never stopped to study it as the complete person, Audra.

She broke the gaze with herself and noticed that the crack in the mirror distorted her nose, mouth, and neck. It seemed as though she were split in two. Neither part of her features looked right without being attached to its other half. "I'm reaching new lows, studying myself in a broken mirror," she thought.

Audra's glance again moved up to the reflection of her crystal green eyes. She noticed a shimmer in them that she hadn't noticed before. Audra felt an immediate sense of hope. "Cracks and all, I like what I see," Audra said quietly. "Here I am with a broken reflection, but I really like what I see."

Once again, Audra moved her focus from her eyes down to her nose; she was stunned to see that the distorted figure in the mirror was gone, along with the crack. She blinked several times, thinking she must be seeing things, or not seeing things. Again, she looked at the mirror, and now her reflection was perfect. No crack.

Audra was filled with a sense of peacefulness mixed with curiosity. "What's going on here? I feel like Alice in Wonderland, but I also feel better than I did earlier." She saw for a minute what a weird and amazing set of experiences she had been having in the last few days.

A thought jumped into Audra's mind. "I guess I'm perfectly imperfect! Even when I saw myself in pieces, I was okay with what I saw."

Audra knew this was a big step for her. She had always felt "less than" or not good enough. She often wished to be able just to accept herself, but she never succeeded. Audra's curiosity turned into elation. "I have a lot to offer and I really don't have to settle," she proclaimed.

Another breakthrough. Audra knew this was another step in her relationship journey. "Lily has to hear about this right now," Audra thought as she grabbed her jacket and ran out of the office.

The Dancing Koi was awash in the late day sun. The metallic door sign glittered, which made Audra smile. "I've grown to love this place," Audra thought. As she opened the door, the electronic gong announced her arrival, which was another comfortably familiar sensation. Several seconds later, Lily appeared from the back of the shop. "Come on in, Audra. What's going on?" Lily asked as she guided Audra into the sun-washed shop.

"Do you have a couple of minutes to talk? I just had another huge experience I have to tell you about it," Audra said excitedly. "I don't really know what's happening with me, but I am starting to just go with it."

"I have a client right now, but let me see if she's okay with having you join us," Lily replied as she walked toward the privacy screen. Lily appeared a moment later and said, "Come on back. Tanya is fine with having you here."

Audra wondered whether this client was the same Tanya she had known several years earlier. Tanya was one of those people Audra had always wanted to get to know better, but she had never made the effort to do so. When Audra peered behind the screen, she saw that it was indeed the same Tanya.

"It's great to see you," Audra said. "Small world and funny that we both found Lily."

"She's amazing, isn't she?" Tanya replied. "This is an independence move for me." Audra was amazed that Tanya was there for exactly the same reason she was. "I just ended another loser relationship," Tanya sighed.

"One more eerie similarity," Audra thought.

Lily went back to work on Tanya's tattoo. Audra noticed that it was a splendidly colored oriental design. "What is that?" Audra asked. "It's beautiful."

"It's 'Houli,' the Chinese symbol for vitality, vigor, and life force," replied Tanya. "I wanted a reminder of who I really am. Seems like I have a tendency to forget it." As Tanya spoke, Audra realized that for the first time in her life, she was feeling some of that life force.

Audra started to think she was intruding on a private moment, and besides, she wanted a moment to think. "I'm sorry I interrupted your session. I'll let you work and I'll catch up with you later, Lily," Audra said.

"Don't worry about it. I'm free after I finish this part of the tattoo. It should only be about ten minutes. Why don't you grab a cup of tea up front and wait for me?" Lily replied.

Audra was relieved that she would have the chance to tell Lily about the mirror. She walked to the front of the salon, poured herself a cup of green tea, and sat in the overstuffed lounge chair. She closed her eyes and recalled her image in the cracked mirror. Several minutes later, Tanya and Lily appeared from behind the screen.

"Don't you love it?" Tanya asked as she showed the tattoo to Audra. "One more session and we'll be done."

"I'm totally jealous. It's a long story, but we're having trouble with mine," Audra replied.

"Well, good luck," Tanya said. "Seems like we have a lot in common. Let's try to get together." Audra wanted to get to know Tanya. She realized how few people she was really close to.

"I'll send you an email. What's your address?" Audra asked.

"It's 'tbirdflies at zerospot dot com,'" Tanya said.

"Great. I'll definitely connect," Audra replied as she wrote down Tanya's address. "See you soon."

After Tanya left the salon, Lily joined Audra for a tea break. "Busy day. I'm doing some fun body art. I love my job," Lily said.

After taking a long sip of tea, Lily asked, "So what got you so excited?"

"I felt something shift," Audra said. She proceeded to tell Lily all of the details surrounding the cracked mirror experience. "After I saw that I was okay with a less than perfect me, I realized I have sold myself short for most of my life," she continued. "I have settled for most of my relationships because I didn't think I deserved more. I do deserve more. I know that," Audra claimed.

Lily held her white china teacup in both hands. She placed the cup on the coffee table and took Audra's hands in hers. Audra noticed the warmth in Lily's hands from holding the hot cup. "I believe you're ready for more of the dragonfly," Lily said softly. "I have time. Let's try."

Lily filled the tattoo machine with pearlescent blue ink and began working on Audra's dragonfly. Lily meticulously filled in the dragonfly's tail, then changed ink colors to start on the dragonfly's body. She placed the machine in position and immediately felt the familiar resistance. Once again, she was unable to continue. "I'm so sorry, Audra. We just can't do anymore yet," Lily said.

Lily sensed Audra's disappointment. "Remember, Audra," Lily said soothingly. "This is a journey. You've taken another step and you've uncovered some important pieces. Please continue."

Lily escorted Audra to the door and opened it without saying a word. Audra left the salon and stood on the sidewalk for a moment where she wondered, "Now what?" She turned to walk back to the office, glad for the distraction of work to put all of this out of her mind.

Lily: *Audra has had three important discoveries in this chapter. Take a look; then comment on each to uncover your own truth.*

Discovery 1: Audra realized that she never really looked at herself when she gazed into a mirror. Take a minute to look into your eyes in a mirror. What do you see, and how does it feel?

Discovery 2: When Audra connected with her true self in the cracked mirror, she liked what she saw, cracks and all. As you're looking in the mirror, look for what you like in the reflection. Describe what happens for you as you do this.

Discovery 3: As Audra's new awareness surfaced, she realized she had a lot to offer someone else, and that she didn't have to settle for less than what she deserved. As you read that discovery, what was your reaction? Have you ever settled for less than you deserve?

Chapter Four

UNDERFOOT

The sun was setting, casting long shadows across the front porch. Audra stepped outside and noticed that the air was eerily still. She stepped off the front porch and walked across the lawn, watching the neighborhood children play. Suddenly, she noticed a pond in front of her next-door neighbor's house she had never seen before.

Audra's gaze fixed on the pond's surface, which seemed to be bubbling. The water started to boil, steam rising from its surface. Hundreds of koi fish jumped out of the pond and formed a moving cloud that surrounded Audra. She tried to run back to her house, but she was held back by the swarming school of fish.

The alarm clock jolted Audra from her nightmare. She felt panicky and fought to catch her breath. "What was *that* about?" she thought. Her panic subsided and she slowly settled herself. "I need a run," Audra thought as she sat up in bed. "That always clears my head. If I hurry, I can take the water route and still get to work on time."

Audra tied back her hair, dressed in her running shorts and jersey, and then chose her lime-green running shoes for today's outing. She grabbed the orange juice out of the refrigerator and took a long swallow directly from the container. Images of swarming koi fish kept entering her thoughts.

It was a perfect morning for a run. The sun was rising over the aspen trees and the air was scented with the fragrance of morning glories. Audra started her run with an easy jog up Sandstone Hill, then followed the bike path to the lake. The route was so familiar that Audra could daydream and even meditate as she ran.

Audra still felt unsettled from her nightmare. She didn't know how to handle so many strange experiences in such a short time. "I'm not sure that I want to uncover much more," Audra thought.

As Audra relaxed into her stride, she started to think about Lily and the Dancing Koi. She realized she was experiencing something completely out of her control. Audra was used to being in control in most areas of her life, so this was a distressing exception.

Each new discovery happened in its own time, without warning or permission. Audra was clearly out of her normal comfort zone. She questioned whether she really had an emotional wall around herself. She thought she had left the dark shadow of her past behind, yet it continued to haunt her and her current relationships. "Ugh," thought Audra as she ran. "Ugh."

Audra's legs began to feel heavy and her stride slowed. She was perplexed because she never got tired on this run. She felt defeated and alone, and she began to slip into self-pity. Suddenly, Audra gasped. She looked at the ground in front of her and saw large words appearing with each stride she took. "You must be kidding!" Audra exclaimed. "Now I've seen everything."

When Audra stopped running, the words disappeared. As she planted her left foot solidly on the path, the word "Compassion" appeared. As her right foot found the path, Audra saw the word "Honesty." The pattern continued, with eight more words being revealed: "Humor," "Responsibility," "Trust," "Family," "Integrity," "Loyalty," "Independence," and "Commitment."

Audra continued running, picking up the pace again. Her legs felt light once more, and she noticed that each time a foot touched the ground, one of the words appeared. Then, the group of ten words began to swirl around her and give her energy. Audra felt more alive than she had since her breakup with Terry. She was surrounded by her ten special words.

When Audra arrived home, the words disappeared. She wrote down the words in her journal so she wouldn't forget them, and she mulled over each one. "Compassion, honesty, humor, responsibility, trust, family, integrity, loyalty, independence, commitment. Why these words?" she thought.

As she studied her writing, Audra realized these were her core values and the values she wanted in her partner. She was both sad and elated. Sad because for so many years, she had ignored what really mattered to her. Elated because this was a new beginning and she had an important new awareness.

Audra realized these ten core principles were absolutely nonnegotiable. She would no longer sell herself short because she wanted to be in a relationship. At that moment, she made a commitment to herself that she would never again compromise those things that were a core part of her just to be in a relationship.

"This is a lot to deal with," Audra thought. "I need to call Faith." That thought surprised Audra, but she followed her intuition.

Faith and Audra had been friends since grade school. For the past year, their relationship had grown distant. Faith had been very vocal about Audra's poor choices in men. She repeatedly told Audra that her actions were self-destructive and that she didn't want to be part of Audra's downward spiral. Audra realized how much she missed Faith, and she wanted to see what Faith thought about the recent surreal events.

"Hi, Faith. It's Audra," she announced. "Do you have a few minutes?"

"Sure, what's up?" Faith replied.

"First, I need to tell you how right you were about Terry. He ended up like all the rest of them. I've been a mess," Audra admitted. "Saying I'm sorry to you isn't enough, but I'll start there. I've been distant and wrapped up in myself."

Audra shared all of her fantastic experiences during the past several days with Faith. There was silence on the other end of the phone as Faith took it all in. "If I didn't know you so well, I'd tell you that you were delusional," Faith exclaimed. "Tattoos, impalas, values, and Lily—amazing."

"So, the dragonfly tattoo is coming along slowly," Audra explained. "With each new awareness, I'm becoming a bit more open, and then Lily can do her work. It's so strange, though, because she always hits another barrier and the tattooing stops."

"I can't believe I'm talking to the same Audra," Faith said.

"And I can't believe all of this is happening," Audra replied. "I can see now that I've put up some pretty serious barriers between me and the world since I was young. I've even had them up with you."

"I know," Faith said softly. "I'm thrilled that you've discovered that now."

"Would you be willing to call me on my stuff if I start slipping backwards?" Audra asked.

"Absolutely, but remember what has happened in the past with us. If I did not agree with you, you often got quite defensive," Faith responded. "I want to support you, yet I don't want to open myself up to having battles with you."

"I feel like I'm different now," Audra said. "For some reason, all of these breakthroughs have removed my need to be right. It's like I'm now looking at my life through a new lens, and I need some support to keep on track. Thanks for believing in me."

"You're so welcome," Faith replied.

"I'll keep you posted on this amazing journey. Thanks again," Audra said.

"Talk to you soon," Faith said.

Audra was moved by how open Faith was to supporting her. She hoped she could herself be there for others and do the same sometime soon. Audra went into the kitchen and put water on for tea. When a familiar fragrance filled the room, she realized the tea she had selected was the same type Lily served her.

"Lily—I've got to tell her about the values," Audra thought. She picked up her purse, phone, and keys and headed to the Dancing Koi.

When Audra rushed into the salon, she found Lily sitting toward the back of the room in a burgundy overstuffed chair. Lily was reading a magazine but looked up as Audra entered.

"Right on time," Lily remarked.

"What? How could you know I would be here? I didn't even know I was coming here today," Audra said.

"I just knew you were ready for another giant discovery," Lily replied. "You've had this energy about you that has been electric. I've been picking up on it."

Audra thought this explanation was a bit strange, but so were many other things in her life right now. "I discovered my values—and the values I want in a relationship today. I was running, and they just appeared. It was as if they surrounded me and could protect me," Audra explained.

Lily thought for a moment, then shared her thoughts with Audra. "Your values will protect you. If you stay true to your core principles, you can't go wrong. If you wait for a partner who shares your values, you're way ahead of the game. Look at the problems you had in every past relationship. Didn't they all occur because you compromised some core part of yourself?"

Audra breathed in Lily's words. "You're right," Audra replied. "I've always compromised on core principles, and it never, ever works. I also realized that I need support to be accountable to myself. I even called a friend whom I had been keeping at a distance. She said she'd be a part of my support system to keep me focused on what's really important to me in a relationship.

Lily smiled broadly as Audra spoke. She was moved by the wisdom she was hearing, yet she knew Audra had quite a bit left to discover on her journey. "I'm really happy and excited for you. You're letting people in, and that big Plexiglas wall you've had around yourself is coming down. You may be tempted to compromise about what you really want, but I encourage you not to," Lily said. "Be true to yourself in all matters and you will experience a joy and fulfillment that far surpasses your wildest dreams."

Audra knew in her heart that Lily was right. She felt strong in her conviction to honor her values. "So what do you think, Lily?" Audra asked. "Can we work on my tattoo?"

"Absolutely," Lily replied.

Once again, Lily prepared the tattoo machine. She rubbed the partially completed dragonfly with alcohol and cleaned the skin around it. Lily carefully completed the dragonfly's body, which was now a pearlescent blue. She refilled the inkwell and began work on the first of the dragonfly's four wings. Audra's skin accepted the shiny purple ink as the wing outline was completed. Yet, just as had happened before, the tattoo machine stopped.

Audra looked at the one perfect outline of a wing and smiled. "I guess this is another beginning, Lily. I have the container, but not the contents."

Lily's heart filled with compassion for Audra. "You're brave and willing," Lily said. "Get back out there and see what's next."

For the first time, Audra left the Dancing Koi with a skip in her step. She was excited about what she had discovered, and hopeful that she would learn what she was supposed to.

Lily: *Audra's making a lot of progress quickly, isn't she? Once you begin your journey to live life differently, your discoveries unfold quickly. Audra had four life-changing discoveries in this chapter. Take a look and see what you think. I'd love to hear your comments about your own discoveries as you read this chapter.*

Discovery 1: Audra is still holding on to the illusion of being in control, yet everything that's happening to her is occurring without her input. What parts of your life are you trying to control? How does this keep you from getting close to others?

Discovery 2: As Audra ran, she discovered her core values: compassion, honesty, humor, responsibility, trust, family, integrity, loyalty, independence, commitment. What values are fundamental to you that you also want in a partner? Take a minute to list them below. What can you do to make sure you stay true to your values?

Discovery 3: Audra realized she needed support to stay true to her values and she asked Faith to support her. Why do you think having a support system is important? Who could you ask to support you in being true to yourself?

Discovery 4: As Lily was continuing with the tattoo, Audra discovered that she now had the container in which she could build a solid relationship, but she still lacked some essential tools. Describe the personal foundation that you're building to assure that you can have a full and loving relationship.

Chapter Five

BLACK DRAGONFLIES

The weather had started to change and fall was in the air. Audra sat on her leather chair in front of her living room window. She noticed that the light outdoors had that golden feel of fall. Audra used to love this time of year because it signaled the start of the holiday season. But this year was different. She dreaded all of the parties and social events since she would be going to them alone.

Three days had passed since Audra's last "discovery" and since she had seen Lily. She sensed that something was about to happen, but she had no idea what it was. Audra peeked at the partially completed dragonfly on her forearm and reminded herself that she was involved in a journey without a map or a timetable.

"All I wanted was a simple tattoo," Audra thought. "I didn't ask for all of this. Maybe I can get it finished somewhere else. Maybe Lily just doesn't know what she's doing. How can it even be possible that my body won't accept the ink?"

Then Audra noticed she was starting to build her protective emotional walls again. They seemed to come up so easily. She could shut down strong or painful emotions by telling herself she didn't really care anyway. Audra had spent a lifetime building walls to protect herself, and she sensed it would take time and practice to keep those walls down.

Audra closed her eyes and took in a long, slow breath. She felt some of the hardness melting away.

"It's incredible just how quickly I can revert back to my old self. I wonder if I'm just doomed to repeat all of my negative patterns. Meditate. That's what I need to do," Audra thought. "Maybe I can get a sense of what's going to happen next if I'm quiet enough." Audra did her best to clear her mind and get centered. She breathed slowly and deeply with the vision of her unfinished dragonfly in her mind.

Audra struggled to relax. It wasn't working. The harder she tried, the more irritated she became. She took one more deep breath. Suddenly, an image appeared before her that made her gasp.

Three black dragonflies appeared on Audra's lap. All of them had broken wings. The smallest dragonfly struggled to take flight but couldn't move. The more it struggled, the more exhausted it became. Audra tried to help the flailing creature. As she took hold of its fragile tail, it dissolved into black ash. She sat back in horror to see that her interference had destroyed the gentle dragonfly.

The larger of the two remaining dragonflies crawled up Audra's arm and settled next to her ear. The small insect whispered into Audra's ear. "You cannot shortcut another creature's journey. We have learned to be content with what is at this moment, and we understand when it's time to stop fighting. There's a delicate balance between the desire to change our circumstances and the ability to be content in just this very moment. You see what happened to the dragonfly that could not do this? Are you interfering with your own journey?"

As quickly as the dragonflies appeared, they melted into the air. Audra had the kind of realization that takes a person's breath away. "I'm struggling, just like the smallest dragonfly. I'm having so much trouble with where I am, and I'm looking for some miracle to happen," she thought. Audra realized the quest she'd been on to complete her tattoo had kept her from enjoying the present moment. The struggle had consumed her joy.

Audra's mind rushed as she had a new awareness. She realized that for most of her life, she had lived either in regret of the past or anticipation of the future. She had been missing the joy available in each moment without even realizing it.

"If I had been present, would I have been able to see my ex as he really was, rather than as I wanted him to be?" Audra wondered. "Have I projected my wants into all the people I know without being able to see who they really are or to accept them as they are?"

Exhaustion started to overcome Audra. How much had she missed by wanting life to be different than it really was? The word "intentional" popped into her mind. "That's something I have not been. I think it means being on purpose—and being present."

Audra shifted in her chair and continued to think about that word. Intentional. "I think this is a big part of why my relationships have not worked. I have not been able just to be in that moment. I'm always on to the next thing without taking in what's in front of me." At that moment, Audra knew she was on to something big, but she wasn't quite sure what it was. "I'm going to check in with Lily on this one," Audra said. She grabbed her purse and headed out the door.

As Audra walked down the busy street, she noticed how aware she was. The breeze felt cool against her skin, the sun warmed the top of her head, and the smell of baking bread oozed out of the Danish bakery. "This is what being intentional is. My senses are really working," Audra thought.

When Audra arrived at the tattoo shop, Lily said, "I've been waiting for you."

"You're amazing, Lily. I just decided to come see you," Audra said.

"Call it a sixth sense," Lily said. "What's happened?"

"I had a vision of black dragonflies that accepted their imperfections. Actually, one of them didn't, and in trying to help it be different than what it was, I destroyed it," Audra commented. "And then I realized that I was completely unaccepting of my imperfections and the imperfections of others. I've been so busy wishing for things to be different, with work and with relationships, that I've been missing the joy hidden in what is."

"That's a big discovery, Audra," Lily replied. "Think of how this can relate to your journey to be ready for a relationship."

"But I'm not looking for a relationship," Audra said abruptly. "I came to you to get a tattoo to declare my independence—to say that I don't need a relationship."

"Audra," Lily said gently, "it's not about need, and it may not be about an external relationship. What about the relationship with yourself? Isn't that what you're healing?"

That simple question stunned Audra. "It is about the relationship with myself. Until I have that, I guess relationships with all others are affected," Audra said with resignation.

"This clearing and discovering will affect you in ways you cannot imagine," Lily said gently. "Let's see if you've opened up any more. Let me get my equipment."

The buzzing sound of the tattoo machine sounded strangely comforting to Audra. Lily continued work on the delicate dragonfly. She was able to complete the outlines of two more wings before the tattoo machine stopped working.

Lily apologized to Audra for not being able to complete more of the tattoo. Lily wasn't surprised, but she felt sad about Audra's struggle. Lily worked to support her without inhibiting her.

"I expected this to happen," Lily said. "I knew this was just another piece."

"I don't feel complete, but I feel ready to be complete, if that makes sense," Audra responded.

"I'm happy for you, and pleased that you're moving forward," Lily said. "I know this has been strange because your life has been mostly predictable. I'd like to share a reflection I was inspired to write as I began my journey of self-awareness. I titled it, 'I Hadn't Planned This.'"

Lily softly read the poem to Audra:

I hadn't planned this.

But before me slammed open a new window.

It wasn't the window I would have chosen.

Mine was just to the left.

The window in front was obscured by mist.

I thought I saw objects as the mist started to clear.

But it wasn't what I expected

Because, you know, I hadn't planned this.

My life had been scripted.

I knew the plays, the players, and the moves.

I journeyed with courage,

Because things were going according to my plans.

And here, after all these years,

My breath was halted from fear.

There was now a window where control was not mine.

I really did not plan this.
I closed my eyes to will it away
Yet the view became clearer and I leaned out that window.
“I need to know more about this,” I thought—
“This really wasn’t as I had planned.”
Why could I not go back to a time
When there were fewer choices, and each choice clear?
Did I dare to cross into that unknown place
Where there is no guarantee—no path clearly marked?
There was no question—
The window was before me.
From a life of well-rehearsed scripts,
Could I dare take this risk?
I hadn’t, couldn’t, wouldn’t plan this.
Yet a small tickle formed in my chest.
Was it joy—a spark of anticipation?
My feet started to move, as my mind yelled, “Beware!”
I saw myself climb through that window.
I hadn’t planned this.
All around me were more paths, more joy,
And unlimited opportunities to explore.
The soft sand supported my innocent feet.
The air embraced me with its welcoming touch.
I felt guided to put one foot in front of the other
And trust that this unplanned journey would be my boldest.
I explored. I sought. I grew.
I felt more alive than ever before.

I dared. I challenged. I discovered I'm fully alive.

And yet, I hadn't planned this.

What lessons lie on life's unexplored paths?

How many have I passed by for fear of change?

Can I risk, err, conquer,

Begin, and change,

Opening to all things I did not plan?

Audra reached out and touched Lily's hand. She realized she was on an unplanned journey that would indeed be her boldest. No words were exchanged as Audra left the shop and headed home.

Lily: *Audra moved from struggling to acceptance in this chapter. At the beginning of the chapter, she seemed concerned not to have her path clearly marked. Yet, by the end, she seemed to be in acceptance about being okay with what is, in the present moment. Audra had four life-altering discoveries in this chapter. I'd love to hear your comments about how you relate to Audra's most recent insights.*

Discovery 1: Audra realized that she can't shortcut the journey to self-discovery. Think about how you feel about your own journey. Are you in acceptance of it, or are you struggling against it?

Discovery 2: Audra realized that she has not been intentional or able just to be content in the present moment. Are you able to practice being intentional and accepting of where you are right at this moment? Describe your reaction to this concept.

Discovery 3: As Audra talked to Lily, she realized she had to have a relationship with herself before she could have a relationship with someone else. What is your relationship with yourself like? Are there some areas you'd like to improve?

Discovery 4: I read my poem, "I Hadn't Planned This," to Audra. How does this poem relate to your life?

____

____

____

____

____

____

____

____

Chapter Six

THE STILL, SMALL VOICE

Work had been easier for Audra since her last visit to Lily. She was more accepting of her coworkers, and she felt more confident in her abilities to do a great job. She also experienced a calm that surprised her.

"My journey with Lily has really changed my work perspective," Audra thought. "Who would have known?"

Audra was grateful there hadn't been any new revelations in the past week, yet she accepted that she was not yet finished with her work. Several people had remarked about the incomplete tattoo on her forearm. Audra's response was always the same, "It's a work in progress, like I am."

As the workday ended, Audra decided she wasn't ready to go home, and she'd like to treat herself to a movie. She shut down her computer, checked her voicemail one last time, and left her office.

Audra decided to take a different route home this evening, so she could walk by the movie theater. As she passed the theater, she noticed *The Road to Paradise* was playing. The critics were very favorable about the film's plot and actors, so Audra decided to see it.

After entering the theater, Audra stopped at the concessions counter for her usual movie treats—a small popcorn without butter and a diet soda. Then Audra entered the dimly lit theater and found a seat on the aisle. No one sat next to her and she hoped it would stay that way.

Several minutes later, the pre-movie advertising began. The first message was an advertisement for the National Center for Peace. Audra was drawn in by the presence of two young children playing together. Their clothing revealed that they were from two different Middle Eastern countries, yet they laughed and played together.

The children stopped their play and started to discuss how much they had in common. The smaller child remarked that his daddy didn't like people who were different. A quote from Albert Einstein appeared at the bottom of the screen: "You can't solve a problem with the same mind that created it."

Audra took in a long deep breath as she read the quote over again. She realized she needed to have a shift in perception, and she also needed some skills she didn't have to continue her journey of growth.

"Up to now, I've done the best I could," Audra thought. "I know I need a different mindset, or a different mind, to have different relationship outcomes. I'm ready to ask for help right now."

Audra hurried out of the theater before the show began and headed to The Dancing Koi. As she approached, she noticed Lily was sweeping the sidewalk in front of the shop. "Guess who?" Audra said.

"Perfect timing. Come on in. I can't wait to hear about what's happened," Lily responded.

Audra was moved by how welcoming and warm Lily was. She envied the ease with which Lily connected with others, and she hoped she'd have that same gift sometime soon.

Audra started to tell Lily about the revelation she'd had at the movies. Lily interrupted her in mid-sentence. "You've looked to me for validation and guidance on your journey," Lily remarked. "And it's been appropriate. I'd like you to try something different right now."

Audra was taken aback. Lily had been open to listening, but now she seemed to be giving instructions instead. "Don't you want the details?" Audra asked.

"I already know," Lily said softly. "Trust me for a few minutes."

Audra felt complete trust in Lily, so she prepared herself for Lily's guidance. "You were about to tell me that you needed new skills," Lily said. "What you really need now is to be able to be still and just listen. You've had an inner guidance since you were born. As you've gotten older, you've stopped listening to it. This has been one of the reasons why you've ended up in hurtful relationships. Your still, small voice has been trying to direct you, but you haven't given it a chance," Lily continued. "So for this moment, please take a deep breath, be still, and see what comes into your consciousness."

As soft flute music played in the background, Audra relaxed into her chair. She breathed deeply and closed her eyes. Audra could hear the wall clock ticking, and she was aware of traffic noises outside the shop. After several moments, the outside distractions were gone and Audra felt peaceful and relaxed. She sensed some messages being formed in her mind. Thoughts drifted in and out. The messages became more clear: take it slowly; stay in the present; full disclosure; authenticity.

Audra opened her eyes and took a pen and paper out of her purse. She wrote down the words she received, then shared them with Lily. "It looks like these are my next challenges, or should I say, 'opportunities'?" Audra asked.

Lily smiled knowingly. "That is the guidance of your still, small voice," Lily instructed. "See how easy and powerful that was. All you have to do is slow down and breathe. The answers are almost always inside you. The more you practice this skill, the better you'll get. What would you think if I told you that checking in regularly with your inner guidance will change your life?"

"I can imagine how it could," Lily responded. It's been so long since I stopped to check in on anything. I didn't know I could do it."

"So, Audra," Lily continued, "it sounds like you need to focus on taking things slowly, being present, or intentional, telling the whole truth, and being true to yourself. Those are some big pieces."

"It's doable," Audra said. "This is a great checklist if I start dating."

"*When* is more like it," Lily replied. "Now let's get back to the dragonfly."

One more time, Lily set up the tattoo machine and prepared to continue with the project. She thought about how far Audra had come in such a short time. The tattoo machine made its familiar buzzing sound as Lily began her work. She was able to complete the outline of the last wing, along with the head and antennae. When Lily shifted the machine's position to begin filling in the delicate wings, it stopped.

Audra let out a sigh, then laughed. "Why am I not surprised?" she said. "I know. More work."

Audra said goodbye to Lily and continued home.

Even though the route home was familiar, it somehow looked different. Audra noticed that the lights looked brighter, and people she passed seemed friendlier. She sensed she was present in that walk home, and it touched her.

When Audra arrived home, she called Faith and told her about the latest developments. Faith was pleased that Audra was reaching out in a way she never had before. Some amazing things were taking place.

At the end of the conversation, Audra admitted, "I really don't know what I'm supposed to do next. I guess I just trust and let things happen."

"You are amazing," Faith replied.

That night, Audra slept more soundly than she had in years.

Lily: *Audra has made tremendous progress, hasn't she? Think about where she started. She blamed others for her unhappiness, but now she's taking full responsibility. She had four important discoveries in this chapter. What are your reactions to this information?*

Discovery 1: Audra realizes she is becoming more accepting in all parts of her life. Can you see where this is happening to you now?

Discovery 2: Audra was touched by Einstein's quote, "You can't solve a problem with the same mind that created it." How does this idea apply to the work you're doing on your relationship issues?

Discovery 3: Did you notice the tremendous breakthrough when Audra was able to get in touch with and listen to her still, small voice? Take a moment to get your own guidance now. Ask yourself this next question; then sit quietly until the answer is clear: "What additional tools do I need to be able to attract the love I'm looking for?" Write about your answer.

Discovery 4: Audra accepted that she had more work to do before being ready for a relationship. She identified several areas to work on. What do you still need to do?

____

____

____

____

____

____

____

____

____

Chapter Seven

ILLUSIONS

Audra awakened from her nap. She stretched and slowly got up from the couch. It had been almost a week since she had discovered her inner voice. She had been practicing listening quietly each day since she last saw Lily. Before getting ready to go out, she took a moment to get quiet.

The guidance she received was puzzling and soothing at the same time. "You're just about ready to welcome in a relationship. Stay present and true to yourself." Audra had been invited to a party at Faith's house that evening. She wondered whether she might meet someone special there.

"So, what do I really have to offer another person?" Audra asked herself. She reviewed her strengths and felt like she had a lot to offer and that she was quite a catch. Audra smiled at this realization, and she felt like she was in a position where she didn't have to settle anymore.

Audra looked through her wardrobe to pick out an outfit that she thought would reflect her inner strength and sense of self. She selected a cream-colored tunic that flowed over her shoulders and highlighted her petite frame. She chose a pair of chocolate-colored capris, accented with copper studs. She added a scarf and amethyst earrings to complete her outfit. She looked in the mirror and felt wonderful. Audra left for the party, feeling a strong sense of hope and excitement.

When Audra arrived at the party, she was greeted by Faith at the door. "Girlfriend, you look amazing! What have you done?"

"I think it's been all this work with Lily," Audra replied. "I'm feeling stronger and more centered than ever."

"What a transformation. I need some of that," Faith responded.

Faith introduced Audra to several people she had not met before. Audra enjoyed getting to know some new people, which in the past had not been the case. She normally stuck with the people she already knew, but she was determined to expand her horizons.

After a few minutes of conversation, Audra noticed that Faith was talking to a very handsome man. She got up the courage to approach Faith and introduce herself to the stranger.

His name was Keene, and he had an air of confidence and independence. As Audra made small talk with Keene, she noticed that her pulse quickened. She was excited by this new person, but she didn't want to slip into her old patterns of spending all of her time with one person who seemed interesting. That was old behavior, and she wanted to do things differently now.

Audra excused herself and went to greet a few friends. An hour later, Keene approached Audra. "I have to get going—I have another commitment this evening," he said. "But I'm intrigued by you and I'd like to call you, if that's okay."

"I'd like that," Audra replied as she gave Keene her card. Audra wanted to jump for joy, but she managed to keep her composure.

Audra stayed until the end of the party and reviewed her evening as she made her way back home. She felt a major shift in her perspective, and noticed how much she enjoyed being able to connect with people on a deeper level. Life was changing and Audra was enjoying it.

The rest of the weekend passed quickly. When Audra's alarm sounded on Monday morning, she was filled with a sense that life was unfolding in a perfectly imperfect way.

Late morning on Monday, Audra received a phone call from Keene. "I've been thinking about you since we met. Actually, I can't get you out of my mind," he said.

"Thanks. It was fun to meet you," Audra replied.

"Are you available for dinner on Wednesday?" Keene asked.

Audra didn't want to appear too available, and it seemed like the date was too soon. "I'm tied up that night. Any other options?" she replied.

"How about Friday after work?" Keene replied.

"That sounds great. Where and when?" Audra asked.

"How about 7:30 at The Oasis on Broadway?" he said.

"I'll look forward to it."

Audra was thrilled that she was able to maintain some emotional distance. This guy seemed like the real thing, she thought. This time, though, she was going to do it differently.

The remainder of the week flew by, and Audra only thought about Keene twice. That was progress.

On Friday evening, there was a slight chill in the air and the wind was gusting. Audra parked her car across the street from the restaurant and hoped that her hair would stay in place while she dashed across the road.

Keene was waiting inside the door. He smiled brightly as he greeted Audra. "It's great to see you again. I've been looking forward to this evening," he said.

Keene's good looks and welcoming demeanor captivated Audra. She was drawn in by his air of confidence and success. She noticed that he was dressed in Lucky Brand jeans and Dolce & Gabbana shoes, which when combined, spoke money and good taste. Audra began to imagine that Keene could be a great catch. At that moment, Audra felt a strange sensation in her stomach. Keene had some of the qualities of her ex-husband—the looks, the self-assuredness. Audra quickly dismissed the thought because Keene appeared to be much more refined than her ex.

The host escorted Audra and Keene to a quiet table next to the window. Keene stood until Audra was seated. "I'm liking this," she thought.

The conversation flowed between the two. Keene asked all the right questions, but he tended to interrupt Audra before she completed her thoughts. She sipped on her chardonnay as Keene described his job and his travels.

Suddenly, Audra began to feel dizzy and disoriented. "What's happening?" she thought. As Audra tried to reorient herself, she noticed that the room began to spin. She was planted in the middle of the room, and everything around her moved in a fast circle.

Audra began to panic. She looked over at Keene and noticed that her ten value words were floating over his head. One by one, each word disappeared in a puff of smoke, until only two of the values remained: responsibility and humor. The rest were gone, and the room stopped spinning.

"This can't be," Audra thought. She was flooded with feelings. She was sad because Keene was not who she was making him out to be. She was afraid because once again she was attracted to someone who shared so few of her values. She felt excitement on top of all of this because she was actually conscious about what was happening. This awareness had never happened before.

For the rest of the meal, Audra made small talk, but she was distracted by what had occurred.

"It's been great being with you, Audra," Keene said when they had finished eating. "I don't want the evening to end. How about drinks and dancing over at The Rose?"

Audra paused for a moment before she replied, "I've enjoyed your company, too, but I realize that we're looking for different things in our lives. I know there's a perfect person waiting for you. Thanks so much for the evening." Audra paid for half of the bill and rushed out of the restaurant.

She was giddy with this breakthrough. Audra knew that The Dancing Koi was open late on Fridays, so she headed to see her mentor, Lily. Audra rehearsed what she would tell her guide. She wanted to share that she had got the rest of the puzzle pieces. "I need to look at potential relationships through the lens of my values, and not my immediate emotional reactions," Audra said to herself. "This is the way for me to do relationships differently. I'm amazed."

Audra quickly rounded the corner on the familiar street and walked toward the second shop from the corner, which housed The Dancing Koi. She stopped abruptly and gasped when she got to the entrance. The Dancing Koi was not there, and it looked like it had never been there.

Audra looked in at an old delicatessen, where a portly man sliced meat behind the counter. She was stunned and shaken. She had been there so many times recently. Lily had been her guide. Where did she go?

Audra turned around and ran to the corner to make sure she was on the right street. There was no mistake. She was at the right location, but there was no tattoo salon there. Once Audra was able to collect herself, she turned and walked slowly home.

"How could this possibly be? I'm losing my grip on reality," Audra thought. "Did I make all of this up? Am I dreaming? I'm going to be sick."

Her heart was pounding as she climbed the stairs to her apartment. Audra hurried to take off her jacket and see whether there really was an almost completed dragonfly tattoo on her forearm. "I don't know if I can even look at my arm," she thought. "What am I going to do if nothing's there?"

Audra closed her eyes as she pushed up her sleeve. She held her breath, opened her eyes, and saw the completed dragonfly on her arm. The wings were filled in, and the dragonfly shimmered in the soft light of her apartment.

Audra slowly released her breath. "I understand," is all she said.

LILY'S EPILOGUE

So, where did I go? Audra didn't need me anymore, and she needed to trust herself. That last realization she had with Keene was enormous. She needed to look at relationships through a values lens. That was the missing piece.

Audra's journey is one you can follow too, to find the relationship that is perfect for you. Let's look at the process I guided Audra through:

- Understanding her past
- Accepting herself
- Discovering her strengths
- Being intentional and in the present moment
- Uncovering her values
- Developing new skills
- Screening dates based on her values

You can have the same success Audra experienced. Just follow the steps.

I also have some resources if you'd like more support. You can find them at: www.Fit4Love.com. You'll find the tools there to take your own personal journey of discovery.

Thank you for letting me be your guide.

Lily

NEXT STEPS

You now have the tools to find a great relationship. Here are some questions to take you to the next level.

List organizations you can join to find like-minded singles:

____

____

____

____

____

____

____

____

How will you know that someone is a good fit for you?

____

____

____

____

____

____

____

____

List 3 actions you will take to start your personal journey to finding that great relationship?

What could get in the way of finding a great relationship?

NOTES

ABOUT THE AUTHOR

Sheila Paxton is an award-winning coach and entrepreneur. She has been a student of relationships for many years and has over twenty years of experience in coaching individuals with their personal and professional relationships. She has developed an exciting process that assists people in bringing intention into all of their relationships.

In addition, Sheila has twenty years of executive-level experience in business consulting, training, and product development. She has received industry awards for general excellence, best employer, best training product, and most innovative business strategies.

Sheila has been praised as a professional speaker and coach. She was recognized as an influential "training renegade" by *Working Woman* magazine and is a sought-after speaker on business trends and best practices for conferences and executive briefings worldwide. Sheila's clients include executives at Fortune 500 companies, as well as small businesses and individuals.

Sheila was divorced twice before she met the love of her life—her current husband, Orley Paxton. They've been married over twenty-five years and still delight in being with each other. Sheila describes the key to long-term relationship success as a commitment to cherish each other's soul and the agreement to full disclosure and communication along the way.

ABOUT INTENTIONAL RELATIONSHIPS

Intentional Relationships is based in beautiful Boulder, Colorado. The company was launched to help people develop authentic and purposeful relationships in all facets of their lives—romance, personal, and business. The founder and senior coach of Intentional Relationships, Sheila Paxton, draws on her wealth of experience as an award-winning entrepreneur who successfully launched three companies and led operations at seven other firms. Paxton has developed the life-changing program, Fit4Love, and is currently certifying coaches in her methodology.

For more information on Sheila Paxton's services, visit:
www.IntentionalRelationships.com
www.Fit4Love.com

BOOK SHEILA PAXTON TO SPEAK AT YOUR NEXT EVENT

When it comes to choosing a professional speaker for your next event, you'll find no one more respected or successful—no one who will leave your audience or colleagues with such a renewed passion for life, both business and personal—than Sheila Paxton. Since 1993, Sheila has delivered more than 500 inspirational presentations worldwide.

Whether your audience is 10 or 10,000, in North America or abroad, Sheila Paxton can deliver a customized message of inspiration for your meeting or conference.

Sheila's style is to provide humor, stories, and passion that entertains and inspires your audience to achieve extraordinary results.

Contact Sheila Paxton to schedule a complimentary pre-speech interview by phone:

www.SheilaPaxton.com
www.IntentionalRelationships.com
sheila@intentionalrelationships.com
303-961-3940